TAMING SNEAKY FEARS

Leo the Lion's Story of Bravery & Inside Leo's Den: the Workbook

Diane Benoit, MD, FRCPC[1]

and

Suneeta Monga, MD, FRCPC[2]

[1] Professor, Department of Psychiatry, University of Toronto, and Staff Psychiatrist, Hospital for Sick Children, 555 University Avenue, Toronto, Ontario, M5G 1X8, Canada

[2] Associate Professor, Department of Psychiatry, University of Toronto, and Medical Director, Psychiatric Ambulatory Services, Hospital for Sick Children, 555 University Avenue, Toronto, Ontario, M5G 1X8, Canada

◆ FriesenPress

Suite 300 - 990 Fort St
Victoria, BC, V8V 3K2
Canada

www.friesenpress.com

Illustrator: Pia Reyes

We thank The Psychiatric Association at the Hospital for Sick Children
for their financial support of this book, as well as the Psychiatry
Endowment Fund at the Hospital for Sick Children and the Ontario
Mental Health Foundation for their funding of research activities related
to the Taming Sneaky Fears program. We are grateful to colleagues,
parents, and children who have participated in the Taming Sneaky Fears
group treatment program at the Hospital for Sick Children over the
years.

ISBN
978-1-5255-1882-9 (Hardcover)
978-1-5255-1883-6 (Paperback)
978-1-5255-1884-3 (eBook)

1. PSYCHOLOGY, PSYCHOPATHOLOGY, ANXIETIES & PHOBIAS

Distributed to the trade by The Ingram Book Company

Table of Contents

Guidelines on How to Use This Story and Workbook

Taming Sneaky Fears has two parts. Part A, Leo the Lion's Story of Bravery, is a children's story. Part B, Inside Leo the Lion's Den – How to Tame Your Sneaky Fears, is the companion workbook to the children's story. Parents can use the story and companion workbook to help their four- to seven-year-old children who are excessively shy and/or are unable to speak in some social situations, and are anxious and fearful in other situations.

The story is about Leo the Lion, who is afraid of his own roar and is too shy, nervous and scared to speak to other animals and his teachers. Together with his friend, Ellie the Elephant, Leo the Lion learns how to overcome his shyness and his fear of speaking by slowly taming his Sneaky Fears. In the workbook, Leo the Lion (with his mother's help on occasion) shows the reader the steps to take for Taming Sneaky Fears.

We suggest you read out loud with your child *only one story chapter and corresponding Inside Leo the Lion's Den section per day (including completing the recommended exercises to help your child grasp and master the concepts discussed in the story)*, ideally when your child is rested and best able to absorb new information. The workbook should take a little over one week to complete—assuming that you read one story chapter and you and your child complete one *Inside Leo the Lion's Den* section per day. However, do not hesitate to spend more time on a specific story chapter and corresponding *Inside Leo the Lion's Den* section if you think your child needs extra time to absorb the information. Also, expect that it will take your child considerably longer than one week to master the various strategies taught in the workbook to overcome his or her excessive shyness, fear of being seen and heard speaking, and other anxiety symptoms. We suggest you encourage your child to practice each strategy as often as recommended in the *Inside Leo the Lion's Den* sections, while ensuring that your child uses the proper technique. *You are an essential component of your child's success* in mastering the various strategies!

We suggest you read the story and entire workbook on your own before you begin the workbook with your child in order to familiarize yourself with all the concepts and strategies that are presented.

As you read the story and complete the workbook with your child, we also recommend that you:

1. Make Healthy Lifestyle Choices with Your Child

Children who are healthy, exercise regularly, and are well fed and rested have a greater capacity to deal with difficult and stressful situations. Learn to recognize when your child is hungry or tired or sluggish from lack of regular activity. Recognize and rectify those situations to help your child manage his or her behavior, emotions, and difficult or stressful situations with more ease.

2. Actively Look for Spontaneous Acts of Bravery and Use Effective Praise

Notice brave behavior, *however small*, in your child every day and provide effective praise. What makes praise *effective* is:

a) Starting your praise statement with 'You' instead of 'I' and focusing on specific aspects of your child's behavior. For example, telling your child, "You looked at your teacher and smiled at her. That's being brave and I'm so proud of you," is better than, "I like it when you look and smile at your teachers and I would like you to do that more because that makes me happy when you do that." The idea here is to help your child know what he or she did well by praising the desired behavior.

b) Telling your child what *specific behavior* your child just displayed that warrants the praise (the more specific the praise, the more effective; for example, saying, "You did a good job looking at the person's eyes and face" is more effective than a generic and unspecific, "Good job").

c) Praising your child *as soon as possible* after your child displays the brave behavior (the more immediate the praise, the more effective).

Note: Some children enjoy effusive and excited displays of approval. Other children, and in fact, most children who are shy and socially anxious, do not like overt and gushing praise as it often makes them feel that they are in the spotlight. They often prefer subtle praise. So use the style of praising that best suits your child's temperamental or personality traits.

3. Manage Non-Compliant, Oppositional, and Defiant Behavior

Many shy or anxious children have angry outbursts, particularly when they face situations that create anxiety for them or involve a change in their routines. Behavior management strategies, such as those offered in Dr. Phelan's *1-2-3 Magic* (book or DVDs), can be helpful to manage angry outbursts. The more consistent and predictable all parents and caregivers are, the better.

4. Help Your Child Practice Each of the Strategies Leo the Lion and His Friend, Ellie the Elephant, Learn in the Story.

These strategies include:

a) How to Be a Feeling Catcher and use a Body Scan and the Feeling Thermometer

b) How to Be the Boss of My Body by using Spaghetti Arms and Toes, Balloon Breathing, and Imagery

c) How to Be a Trick Catcher and catch the Tricks that Sneaky Fears play (Not Telling the Truth, Exaggerating, and Only Showing the Bad Things)

d) How to Be the Boss of My Brain and use the three Trick Stoppers (Ignore Sneaky Fears, Think Brave Thoughts, and Talk to an Adult)

e) How to Be the Boss of Sneaky Fears by climbing Bravery Ladders (and using all the aforementioned strategies)

We hope that Leo the Lion's story and companion workbook will inspire your child to tame his or her own Sneaky Fears and overcome shyness, fear of speaking, and many other fears!

Additional Suggested Resources for Parents

Huebner, D. *What to Do When You Worry Too Much – A Kid's Guide to Overcoming Anxiety.* Magination Press, 2006.

This is a workbook for children who worry excessively (about situations other than social interactions and using their voice to speak).

Manassis, K. *Keys to Parenting Your Anxious Child (2nd Edition).* Barron's Educational Series, 2008.

This is a book for parents who wish to help their anxious children.

Phelan, T.W. *1-2-3 Magic: Effective Discipline for Children 2-12 (6th Edition).* ParentMagic, Inc., Illinois, 2016.

This is a book to help parents use effective discipline. Also available in two DVDs: *1-2-3 Magic DVD: Managing Difficult Behavior* and *More 1-2-3 Magic DVD: Encouraging Good Behavior.*

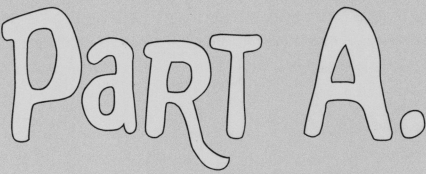

Part A.

Story: Leo the Lion's Story of Bravery

Story Chapter 1.

In a faraway jungle, there was a small lion who lived with his mom, dad, and baby sister. His name was Leo. Leo was small because he was only five years old. Leo was supposed to be brave because he was a lion, King of the Jungle!

But Leo had a big problem.

He almost never felt brave like a lion should. He almost always felt shy, nervous, and scared like a skittish kitty cat.

When Leo was with animals he did not know well, he kept thinking that he would say or do something that would make all the animals laugh at him, make fun of him, and think bad things about him. Leo felt too shy to make new friends.

And Leo had an even bigger problem!

Leo was afraid of his own roar! He kept thinking that his roar sounded too loud and silly. So Leo never spoke to small animals or grown up animals. Even at school, Leo did not speak to his teacher or the other animals.

Leo did not know what to do.

Leo's parents did not know what to do.

Then, one day, Leo's mom told him, "Tomorrow, I'm going to take you to a **Bravery Club** where you'll learn how to be brave about making friends and using your roar."

Leo wanted to learn how to be brave, but he did not want to go to any Bravery Club!

"There's no way I can roar in front of the animals at the Club," he grumbled on his way to his room. He was so upset that he kicked a toy. He even slammed his door extra hard, just to show his mom that he really did not want to go. His tummy started to feel sore, just like it always did when he thought about speaking to animals.

That night Leo had a lot of trouble falling asleep. His brain kept telling him, "All the animals at the Club will think your roar is too loud and sounds silly. If you say something, everyone will laugh at you!"

That made Leo's muscles get all hard and stiff. *Just like uncooked spaghetti noodles before mom cooked them for dinner*, Leo thought. He remembered that when his mom put the hard and stiff uncooked spaghetti noodles in warm water for dinner earlier, they had become soft and wobbly. Leo wished he could make his hard and stiff muscles become soft and relaxed just like cooked spaghetti noodles.

That's when Leo thought about it! *I'll make my muscles get hard and stiff on purpose, like uncooked spaghetti noodles. Then I'll pretend I'm putting them into warm water to make them all relaxed and soft and wobbly, like cooked spaghetti noodles.*

Leo stiffened his toes for a few seconds to make them hard and stiff like uncooked spaghetti noodles. Then he relaxed them and pretended to slide them into warm water.

Then he stiffened his arms, as tight as he could. His arms felt a little sore because they were so tight. And then he pretended to put his arms into nice, warm water. That made his arms feel so relaxed.

I'm doing

Spaghetti Arms and Toes

right now, Leo thought as he giggled a little.

Leo liked how soft and relaxed his arms and toes felt now, so he decided to do Spaghetti Arms and Toes with all his other muscles. He stiffened his legs and thighs for a few seconds and then relaxed them. He stiffened his neck and his face and then relaxed them. Then he tightened his whole body, like he was a giant uncooked spaghetti noodle! And then he relaxed his whole body and thought, *I can make my muscles get hard and stiff or get soft and relaxed if I want to. I can be the Boss of My Body!*

Story Chapter 2.

Just as Leo tried falling asleep again, his brain started to think, *If you use your roar at the Bravery Club tomorrow, everyone will laugh at you!*

And sure enough, that thought made Leo's muscles get hard and stiff like uncooked spaghetti noodles. Even his tummy started to feel sore and his heart started knocking hard and fast in his chest.

That's when Leo called out to his mom. She came in, carrying baby Lilly who had just fallen asleep in her arms. Leo caught a sweet and fruity whiff as his mom sat next to him on the bed. She put baby Lilly on the bed.

Leo snuggled into his mom and breathed in the sweet and fruity smell on her fur and apron. He told his mom how he relaxed his muscles with Spaghetti Arms and Toes, "But I can't make my tummy un-sore and my heart slow down."

Leo's mom gently stroked his forehead, then placed her paw on his and said, "Look at baby Lilly's tummy when she's relaxed and sleeping, Leo. See how her tummy looks like it's a balloon that fills up with air when she breathes in and lets all the air out when she breathes out."

Leo said, "Baby Lilly is Balloon Breathing!"

Leo's mom said, "Right! Try doing **Balloon Breathing** and it'll help you get so relaxed that you'll be able to sleep."

Leo tried Balloon Breathing. He closed his eyes. He took a slow breath in and made his tummy go up and fill up with air, just like a balloon. Then he slowly breathed out and made all the air go out of his belly-balloon. Leo did Balloon Breathing a few times and the sore feeling in his tummy went away. His breathing and his heart slowed down, just right. Leo even started feeling a little sleepy because his whole body felt so relaxed.

Leo felt a **nice and warm** breeze gently blowing through the open window of his den. He could hear the soft whooshing and flapping sounds his window curtain made as it slowly rose and fell in the gentle breeze. He breathed in the sweet fruity smell of his mom's fur and apron and the lovely vanilla ice cream fragrance of the jungle flowers the gentle breeze carried into his bedroom.

Leo's mom said, "When you do Balloon Breathing, close your eyes and make your brain think that you're relaxing in the shade under your favorite tree. The air smells sweet and clean. The grass feels nice and cool under your body. You hear the soft swishing of the leaves in the tree above you; that sound is so relaxing. A warm breeze blows gently on your face and feels so nice. You feel calm, safe, and relaxed."

Leo started yawning. His mom said, "Leo, that was Imagery you just did. Imagery is when you close your eyes and make your brain think of relaxing in your calm and safe place under your favorite tree. When you do Imagery and Balloon Breathing *together*, that makes you the boss of your body and your brain."

Leo thought,

I'm the boss of my body and my brain right now,

just as his mom gave him a kiss good night and said, "Sweet dreams, my brave little lion."

Leo closed his eyes and did more Balloon Breathing and Imagery. In no time, Leo started dreaming sweet dreams.

STORY Chapter 3.

When Leo arrived at the Bravery Club the next day, one of the animals smiled at him and came to sit next to him. Her name was Ellie the Elephant. She told Leo, "I'm five and three-quarters years old." Ellie giggled a lot and when she did, she lifted her trunk all the way up and her beautiful big flapping ears seemed to giggle with her.

Soon the Club leader, Ms. Priya the Panther, introduced herself. She curled and uncurled her long tail slowly and with it, she pointed at all the animals, one at a time, inviting them to say what made them feel shy, nervous, or scared.

Leo learned that all the animals were shy, nervous, or scared about things like sleeping by themselves, answering questions in front of the class, being on stage for the school concert, being away from their parents, the dark, storms, and many, many other things.

When it was Ellie the Elephant's turn to speak, she said,

"I'm scared of making mistakes.

If I can't do something perfectly perfect the first
time, then I won't even try."

Then it was Leo's turn.
Ms. Priya uncurled her long tail toward Leo and asked,
"How old are you, Leo?"

Right away, Leo's body started to feel like a giant, uncooked spaghetti noodle. His muscles felt all hard and stiff. His throat started to feel like something was squeezing it so tight that his voice was stuck and would not come out.

Leo knew that he had to do Spaghetti Arms and Toes, Balloon Breathing, and Imagery right away to relax his body. And he did just that. So when Ms. Priya said, "Show me with your paw how old you are," Leo was able to stretch his paw and show five tiny claws. But Leo's throat still felt squeezed and his voice felt stuck. He wished he knew what to do to unsqueeze his throat and unstick his voice.

Before Leo could think more, Ms. Priya told all the animals, "Your worst fears are like wild and scary beasts that trick your brain. One trick is to sneak scary thoughts in your brain. They make your brain think that you can't do things. They can make your throat feel so squeezed that your voice gets stuck and won't come out. They are very tricky and very, very sneaky."

Leo's head snapped up and his eyes widened. *That's exactly what's happening to me*, he thought.

Leo knew that his worst fears were his fear of making new friends because he was shy, and his fear of animals seeing and hearing him roar. He imagined his worst fears were two huge wild jackals that kept snarling, hissing, and showing their big and sharp teeth. Their grayish fur was all twisted and smelled really stinky, like rotten garbage.

These mean and stinky wild jackals liked playing tricks on Leo. They kept sneaking scary thoughts in Leo's brain with their growling voices, "Your voice sounds so loud and weird. If you use your voice everyone will laugh at you!" These thoughts made Leo's muscles get hard and stiff like uncooked spaghetti noodles, his tummy feel sore, his heart knock hard and fast, his breathing get all choppy, and his throat feel so squeezed and tight that his voice got stuck and would not come out.

Ms. Priya is right, Leo thought, *these wild and scary jackals are very tricky and very, very sneaky!*

That's when Leo thought about it: *Sneaky Fears! That's what I'll call you.*

I'll call you my Sneaky Fears!

Ms. Priya continued, "Your worst fears, these wild and scary beasts, need to be tamed. Taming them is the only way you can unsqueeze your throat and unstick your voice. Taming them is the best way you can become brave."

Leo blinked. He had never known that to unsqueeze his throat, unstick his voice, and become brave all he had to do was tame his Sneaky Fears! Leo thought, *Taming Sneaky Fears is a great idea!*

But Sneaky Fears did not think that being tamed was a great idea at all. They started snarling and shouting over Ms. Priya, "Don't listen to Ms. Priya! No one can tame us. We'll always keep your voice stuck. We'll never stop!"

Leo started to believe Sneaky Fears. Sneaky Fears could be so convincing.

Leo's Sneaky Fears snickered and whispered to each other, "Look at Leo! Our tricks are working great. Every time we sneak scary thoughts in Leo's brain, he believes they're true!"

Leo's Sneaky Fears were jumping around and doing all sorts of little happy dances. They were giving each other high fives and could not stop laughing. They kept telling each other, "We make Leo's throat feel all tight and squeezed, and his voice all stuck, and his body all shy, nervous, and scared because we're the boss of Leo's body! Leo will never be able to figure out our tricks because we're the boss of Leo's brain too!"

But Sneaky Fears did not know who they were dealing with! They had not realized that Leo was a really smart lion, even though he was small. And they had not realized how much Leo wanted to be brave.

Leo decided to be the boss of his body. He did Spaghetti Arms and Toes, Balloon Breathing, and Imagery. After he calmed his body down, Leo was able to think more clearly. He thought about what his Sneaky Fears said about his voice sounding so weird that every animal would laugh at him. Leo remembered that his parents had told him that his roar sounded great, like the roar of a King of the Jungle. Leo knew that his parents only told him the truth. Leo shook his head as he realized, *My Sneaky Fears are Not Telling the Truth!*

Just like that, Leo had figured out that Not Telling the Truth was a trick that Sneaky Fears played on his brain. Leo had become a Trick Catcher!

That's when Leo decided, *I'm going to Ignore Sneaky Fears and Think Brave Thoughts, like "I can do it!"* And with that, Leo the Trick Catcher Lion had figured out two of the best Trick Stoppers:

Ignore Sneaky Fears and Think Brave Thoughts.

Leo imagined telling his Sneaky Fears, *You think you're so wild and scary and tricky and sneaky, but I'll tame you!* Leo imagined catching his Sneaky Fears, putting them on leashes, and giving them a bubble bath to get the stink out!

In the midst of their jumping around and little happy dances, Leo's Sneaky Fears jerked to a sudden stop in mid-air. Their bodies plopped down to the ground. They looked at each other's necks with their new leashes on. Their eyes got big like they were popping out of their sockets. They could not believe a little five-year-old lion had just caught them and figured out their trick of Not Telling the Truth. They never thought Leo could discover that Ignore Sneaky Fears and Think Brave Thoughts were two powerful Trick Stoppers.

Leo was so busy being the boss of his body and his brain, being a Trick Catcher, using Trick Stoppers, and putting Sneaky Fears on leashes, that he did not realize that he whispered out loud, "Got you, Sneaky Fears!"

But Leo had whispered loud enough for Ms. Priya and the animals to hear. Leo saw that no one laughed or made fun of how his whisper sounded. That's when Leo became sure of it! What his Sneaky Fears had said about his voice sounding so loud and weird that all the animals would laugh was not even true. His Sneaky Fears had been using their trick of Not Telling the Truth all along!

At that moment, Leo felt brave enough to smile at Ellie the Elephant. That made Ellie's eyes sparkle like bright stars in the night sky!

STORY Chapter 4.

On their way out after the Club meeting, Ellie approached Leo and said, "Hi."

Leo wanted to say hi back, but his Sneaky Fears growled, "Don't say hi! Ellie the Elephant is going to think that your voice is too loud and sounds weird."

Right away, Leo's throat squeezed up and his voice got stuck. His muscles were all tight like uncooked spaghetti noodles.

On their leashes, Leo's Sneaky Fears were laughing and joking, "Look! Our trick of Not Telling the Truth is still working!" They started giving each other high fives and doing their little happy dances.

But Leo really wanted to be brave and say hi to Ellie. Leo figured out quickly that his Sneaky Fears were trying to be the boss of him. Leo decided that *he*, not Sneaky Fears, was going to be the boss of his body and his brain. Leo did Spaghetti Arms and Toes, Balloon Breathing, and Imagery to be the boss of his body. And then he was able to use his new Trick Stoppers; Ignore Sneaky Fears and Think Brave Thoughts, and became the boss of his brain.

But when Leo's Sneaky Fears saw that Leo was becoming the boss of his body and his brain, they freaked out! "We can't let that happen," they told each other, "Let's use our other tricks. There's no way a small lion can figure out those other tricks. No way!"

Leo's Sneaky Fears put their huge mouths with the sharp teeth right in Leo's face and started bothering Leo.

"Your voice sounds weird. If you use your voice, Ellie the Elephant and all the animals in the entire animal kingdom will just laugh and laugh and laugh at you. No one will ever want to be your friend. Ever!"

Leo's muscles started to feel hard and stiff like uncooked spaghetti noodles again. His heart started knocking in his chest and his breath got all choppy. His tummy started to feel sore and yucky. His throat felt like it was being squeezed and his voice was stuck and would not come out, no matter how much he tried to unsqueeze his throat and unstick his voice.

But Leo did not give up. Leo would not let Sneaky Fears be the boss of him. He was going to be patient and tame his Sneaky Fears!

Leo knew that he needed to calm his body down first, and then he would be able to make his brain think clearly. Leo did Spaghetti Arms and Toes, Balloon Breathing, and Imagery. When his body was calm and relaxed, Leo was able to Ignore Sneaky Fears and Think Brave Thoughts. *I can do it*, he told himself, *I can figure out what other tricks Sneaky Fears are playing on my brain right now*. Leo started to think really hard about the thoughts Sneaky Fears had snuck in his brain.

That's when Leo the Trick Catcher Lion spied the two new tricks! His Sneaky Fears were. . . exaggerating! They were making things sound much, much worse than they really were. Sure, Leo was shy and did not have many friends. But he also knew that Ellie wanted to be his friend. And it could not be true that his voice would be stuck in his throat forever and ever, because he was able to use his voice without any problem when he spoke with his mom, dad, and his baby sister. Leo's Sneaky Fears were Exaggerating! Not only that, but Sneaky Fears were Only Showing the Bad Things! They were not showing any of the good things like how much fun it would be for Leo to play and talk with a new friend! Plus, they were using their old trick of Not Telling the Truth!

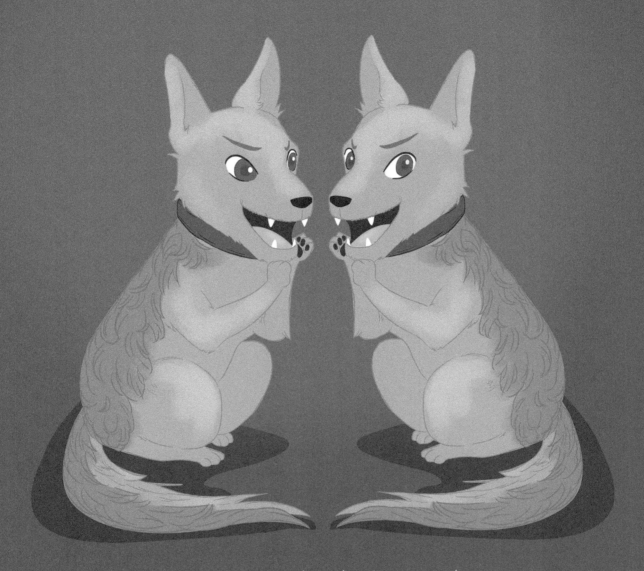

Leo's Sneaky Fears were noticing how close Leo was getting to say hi to Ellie and they did not like that at all. One of Leo's Sneaky Fears whispered to the other, "Leo won't be able to figure out that we like to be kept a secret. When small animals Talk to an Adult that makes it impossible for us to be wild and scary. No way Leo the Lion can figure that out. No way!"

Leo's other Sneaky Fears frowned and hissed, "Shhhh! Don't whisper so loud! Leo might hear and then he'll know that Talk to an Adult is a powerful Trick Stopper that tames us super fast. Shhhh!"

Just then, Leo saw his mom. He ran to her and told her all about what his Sneaky Fears were doing. Leo's mom said something that surprised him: "Leo, you just figured out another really powerful Trick Stopper and that's to Talk to an Adult—like me or your dad, or any other adult you trust. Use your other Trick Stoppers, and you'll be able to say hi to Ellie."

Just as Leo was using his Trick Stoppers, his throat started to unsqueeze and his voice got unstuck enough that Leo was able to whisper to Ellie, "Hi."

Leo's Sneaky Fears could not believe it! On their leashes, they were running in circles and whimpering, "Oh no! We know only three tricks and Leo has figured all of them out. If Leo keeps practicing being the boss of his body and his brain, being a Trick Catcher, and using his Trick Stoppers, our tricks won't work anymore. We'll be tame. Oh no, oh no!"

Ellie giggled and asked Leo if he wanted to come to her house for a play date. Leo told her in a soft voice, "Yes. I'll ask Mom if it's okay." Ellie's face brightened and her eyes sparkled like bright stars in the night sky again!

Just like that, by being the boss of his body and brain, being a Trick Catcher and using his Trick Stoppers, Leo had unsqueezed his throat and unstuck his voice. And he had made a new friend!

Story Chapter 5.

hen Leo arrived at Ellie's house for their play date and Ellie opened the door, Leo could smell a wonderful sweet aroma. On the kitchen countertop, Leo could see a batch of cupcakes decorated in the most dazzling red, orange, yellow, green, blue and purple glitter frosting. Leo's mouth watered and his tummy growled in a good way.

Ellie's mom welcomed Leo. She told Leo and Ellie, "You can each have a cupcake, but first, I want you to come with me to check on Ellie's big brother, Elliot."

Elliot the Elephant was in his bed, sick with the flu. His nose was all red and swollen and really runny. Big garbage cans sat next to Elliot's bed and were spilling over with used tissues. Dozens and dozens of unopened tissue boxes were stacked up next to Elliot's bed. Leo thought, *When an elephant's nose gets runny, you need lots and lots of tissues!*

Ellie's mom explained, "I have to check how much fever Elliot has." She showed Ellie and Leo a fever thermometer, "You see all the numbers on the fever thermometer?"

Leo could see that the fever thermometer had numbers going from 0 at the bottom to 10 at the top.

As Ellie's mother checked Elliot's fever, she said, "Each number tells me how much fever Elliot has. If Elliot's fever is a 0 at the bottom of the fever thermometer, that means he has no fever at all. If Elliot's fever is a 1 or 2 toward the bottom of the fever thermometer, that means he has just a little bit of fever. But if Elliot's fever is a 5 or more toward the middle, or all the way up the fever thermometer at a 9 or 10, that means Elliot's fever is way too high. And then I have to do something to make the fever thermometer go down."

That gave Leo an idea, *I could use a thermometer to decide how much I'm feeling something, like how shy or nervous or scared or sad or mad I'm feeling.* He decided to talk to Ellie about it.

Ellie's mom said, "Right now, Elliot's fever is a 1 on the thermometer, so Elliot is okay." She pointed at Ellie and Leo with her trunk and said, "Alright, you two, Elliot needs to rest until his fever gets all the way down to 0. You can go to the kitchen to eat a cupcake and then you can go play in Ellie's room."

On their way to the kitchen, Leo told Ellie about his idea of using a thermometer to tell how much he was feeling something. He said, "We could call it a Feeling Thermometer! That way, we'll be able to tell when we're feeling just a little nervous or scared, like a 1 or a 2 on the Feeling Thermometer."

Ellie said, "Like when my cousin Eleanor the Elephant jumps out from behind a chair and shouts, 'Boo!' That's just a little scary."

Leo said, "Right! And when we're 5 or more on the Feeling Thermometer for nervous or scared, that means it's too high. It means we're way too upset. And when we're that upset, we can't think clearly. That's when we need to get our Feeling Thermometer down to a 0 or a 1."

As Leo and Ellie were choosing their cupcakes and Ellie got juice boxes, Ellie asked, "But how do you make your Feeling Thermometer go down?"

Leo knew the answer! He said, "You have to be the boss of your body and make your body calm down even if it doesn't want to calm down!"

As they ate their snack and drew pictures, Leo told Ellie about how Spaghetti Arms and Toes, Balloon Breathing, and Imagery could make a Feeling Thermometer for shy or nervous or scared go all the way down to a 0 or 1!

STORY Chapter 6.

After Leo and Ellie finished their snack and their drawings, they went to Ellie's room to play. Ellie ran to her bunk bed and plopped herself down on the bottom bunk.

Leo could see a present wrapped in shiny paper and sparkly ribbon and bow on the top bunk. He asked, "Ellie, is that a present?"

Suddenly, Ellie's eyes looked all sad. Her face and beautiful big ears became all droopy. The tip of her trunk thumped to the floor. Her shoulders slumped. She lowered her eyes. She spoke in such a soft voice that Leo had to stretch his neck and crane his head toward Ellie to be able to hear.

"Well, it's a present for me. But my mom said I need to climb up the bunk bed ladder to get it."

Leo said, "So why don't you?"

One of Ellie's legs started bouncing up and down and her bed made little cracking and creaking sounds. Ellie hated to admit it: "I'm too scared to climb the ladder."

Ellie grabbed something from under her pillow and showed it to Leo. "It's a drawing I made of my own Sneaky Fears. I call her Missy Mistake. Whenever I try climbing a step of the ladder, even just the bottom step, Missy Mistake points her long crooked fingers at me and screams, 'Don't try anything new, Ellie the Elephant! You'll make a really big, like a M O N U M E N T A L mistake! You'll never be able to climb the ladder! Never! It's way too high!'"

Leo could see sweat on Ellie's forehead as she said, "I just can't do it."

Leo asked Ellie how high she was on her Feeling Thermometer right now when she thought of Missy Mistake bothering her.

Ellie thought for a few seconds. Her eyes widened and she gasped, "A 9! That's way too high! I need to get my Feeling Thermometer down!"

Ellie did Spaghetti Arms and Toes, Balloon Breathing, and Imagery.

After Ellie calmed her body down, she was able to think more clearly. She saw right away that Missy Mistake was sneaking scary thoughts in her brain. Missy Mistake was using the only three Tricks that all the Sneaky Fears around the world know: Not Telling the Truth, Exaggerating, and Only Showing the Bad Things.

Leo told Ellie how the Trick Stoppers, Ignore Sneaky Fears, Think Brave Thoughts, and Talk to an Adult, could help stop Missy Mistake from playing tricks on her brain.

Leo then had an idea. He told Ellie, "Pretend the ladder is not just a bunk bed ladder, Ellie. Pretend it's a Bravery Ladder! Each step you climb on your Bravery Ladder makes you more and more brave, and makes Missy Mistake more and more tame. When you've climbed all the way up your Bravery Ladder, you're brave and Missy Mistake is tame!"

Ellie's eyes sparkled, her trunk went all the way up, and her beautiful big ears started flapping happily again. She giggled and said, "If I do Spaghetti Arms and Toes, Balloon Breathing, and Imagery just before I get ready to climb a step, I'll be all calm and relaxed. I'll be the boss of my body! I'll be able to Ignore Missy Mistake and Think Brave Thoughts, like *I can do it*. I *can* climb the step! Missy Mistake won't be the boss of me!"

Missy Mistake did not like the sound of that at all! Missy Mistake was not used to dealing with a brave Ellie. Missy Mistake started screeching at the top of her lungs, "Don't climb! You'll fall! You'll break all your bones and no one will be able to put you back together!"

Ellie's Feeling Thermometer started to shoot up and got way too high again.

But just like Leo, Ellie really wanted to be brave. Ellie started doing Spaghetti Arms and Toes, Balloon Breathing, and Imagery. After Ellie made her Feeling Thermometer go all the way down to a 0, she was able to Ignore Missy Mistake, and Think Brave Thoughts, like *I can do it!*

Ellie stood up, approached the ladder, put one foot on the first step, then put her other foot on the first step.

Ellie had climbed the first step of her Bravery Ladder.

Missy Mistake could not believe it! She started wagging her long, crooked fingers at Ellie and screeching as loud as she could, "Get down! Get down, I said! You're going to fall and break all your bones. You'll stay broken forever and ever."

Big beads of sweat were rolling down on Ellie's forehead. Her eyes grew big like full moons. Her face was all scrunched up from fear. Her body shook so much that the ladder was making all sorts of cracking and creaking sounds. Her Feeling Thermometer had shot all the way up to a 10!

Leo could see that Ellie was really nervous and scared. He said, "Ellie, don't let Missy Mistake be the boss of you! Stay on the step and do Balloon Breathing and Imagery."

Ellie did Balloon Breathing and Imagery. Slowly, she made her Feeling Thermometer go down to a 0. When her body was calm, Ellie was able to Ignore her Sneaky Fears and Think Brave Thoughts: *I can do it! I can stay on the step!*

Ellie stayed on the step! After a few minutes on the step, Ellie's body relaxed. Ellie told Leo, "I want to push myself. I want to climb up to the second step." She closed her eyes, did Balloon Breathing, and climbed on the second step.

Missy Mistake did not like that one bit! She wagged her long, crooked fingers close to Ellie's face, almost scratching Ellie's cheeks. Missy Mistake kept screeching even louder than before, "Don't you listen to Leo the Lion! You C A N ' T climb another step! You'll fall and get hurt!"

Ellie's eyes popped wide open. Her whole body started to shake. That made her bed moan, creak, crack, and shake like in an earthquake. Ellie fanned herself with her beautiful big ears. Large beads of sweat were rolling down her face and dropping to the floor in small puddles. Ellie thought she might lose her grip because her body was sweating and shaking so much.

Leo was cheering Ellie on, "Don't let Missy Mistake be the boss of you, Ellie!"

Ellie did not give up. She hung on tight. She did more Balloon Breathing and Imagery until she made her Feeling Thermometer get all the way down to a 0. Ellie had had it with Missy Mistake's pranks! Ellie decided to pretend she was putting Missy Mistake in a pretty purple cage. . . and putting a hot pink cloth on top of it for good measure! And that did it. Missy Mistake finally got quiet!

Ellie was so proud of herself! She had made Missy Mistake quit bothering her. She had climbed all the way to the second step! She had never been able to do that before. She lifted her trunk all the way up and her beautiful big ears started flapping as she giggled and giggled.

Ellie was so excited that she called out to her mom in between giggles. When Ellie's mom came into her room, she gasped. Her eyes widened. Her hands flew to her cheeks. She was speechless for a moment. Then her face broke into a huge smile. She lifted her trunk all the way up and started giggling with Ellie! She approached Ellie, and gave her a nice big hug. "I'm so proud of you, my brave Ellie!"

Later, as he was leaving to go home, Leo told Ellie, "You were so brave climbing two steps of your Bravery Ladder, Ellie! When I get home, I'm going to build my own Bravery Ladder and start climbing each step!"

STORy Chapter 7.

On his way home with his mom, Leo told her about Ellie climbing two steps of her Bravery Ladder and how he would like to build his own Bravery Ladder.

"I'm going to call it My Bravery Ladder for Speaking at School!" he said.

Leo's Sneaky Fears did not like the sound of that at all. Sure, Leo's Sneaky Fears now had leashes around their necks and Leo had given them a bubble bath so their stinky smell was gone, but that did not stop them from wanting to bother Leo. They whispered to each other, "We can't let Leo the Lion climb any Bravery Ladder, because that'll tame us completely."

With their leashes on, Leo's Sneaky Fears tried bothering Leo. "Bravery Ladders are just silly and useless. Plus, a Bravery Ladder for Speaking at School is just *way* too hard to climb. You can't tame us, Leo the Lion. We'll always be the boss of you!"

Right away, Leo told his mom what his Sneaky Fears were saying.

Leo's mom said, "You need to be really patient when you're Taming Sneaky Fears. Your Sneaky Fears don't want to be tamed so they'll throw big tantrums to try and scare you and make you think you can't do it! Don't believe your Sneaky Fears! You *can* tame your Sneaky Fears! If you practice climbing steps of your Bravery Ladder every day, one baby step at a time, your Sneaky Fears will learn faster that you won't let them be the boss of you and you'll be taming them faster!"

With his mom, Leo decided what each step of his Bravery Ladder for Speaking at School would be. Then Leo's mom met with his teacher and showed her all the steps of his Bravery Ladder. Leo's mom told the teacher what Leo needed to do to be the boss of his body and his brain. She showed the teacher how to do Spaghetti Arms and Toes, Balloon Breathing, and Imagery. She told her about the Feeling Thermometer, the Trick Stoppers, and how to be a Trick Catcher.

Leo and his teacher were now ready for Leo to climb the first step of his Bravery Ladder for Speaking at School. When Leo got to school the next day, he and his teacher went to a room, just the two of them.

Leo sat next to his teacher and saw a picture book on the table. Leo's first step on his Bravery Ladder was to name what his teacher was pointing at in the book, and say the word with his lips without using his voice. When the teacher pointed at the picture and told Leo to use his lips without his voice to say the word, Leo's Feeling Thermometer shot all the way up to a 5. Sure enough, Leo's Sneaky Fears started bothering him.

Right away, Leo used Spaghetti Arms and Toes, Balloon Breathing, and Imagery. His body started to calm down. Leo thought, *Okay. I'm the boss of my body. Now, I need to be the boss of my brain.* Leo started to Ignore Sneaky Fears and Think Brave Thoughts. *I can do it, I can use my lips without my voice to say the word.*

And Leo did it!

Leo's teacher told him how proud she was that he was using his lips without using his voice. He had climbed the first step of his Bravery Ladder! She said, "Now, try and climb the second step of your Bravery Ladder and whisper the word."

Leo's Sneaky Fears started to throw a huge fit because they were not getting their way. They did not want Leo to climb another step of his Bravery Ladder. They were yanking on their leashes, throwing themselves on the ground, and making really angry and scary snarls. Leo's Sneaky Fears hissed, "It's way too hard, you won't be able to whisper in front of the teacher!"

Leo's Feeling Thermometer started to go up and up and up.

Leo's Sneaky Fears were jumping with joy. They were giving each other high fives and saying, "We did it! We made Leo's brain think all sorts of scary thoughts. We're still the boss of Leo's brain. Leo really believes that climbing a new step on his Bravery Ladder is way too hard!"

But Leo's Sneaky Fears had forgotten how much he wanted to be brave! Plus, Leo's teacher was there to help him. While his Sneaky Fears were busy playing their pranks on Leo, his teacher reminded him to do Spaghetti Arms and Toes, Balloon Breathing, and Imagery to get his Feeling Thermometer down. After Leo did, he was able to make his brain Ignore Sneaky Fears and Think Brave Thoughts like, *I can do it! I can Ignore Sneaky Fears. I can use my real whisper to answer my teacher's question!*

Leo's body started to relax.

His throat started to unsqueeze and his voice started to get unstuck. Leo used his whisper voice to say the word!

Leo's Sneaky Fears froze in mid-air. A thump could be heard when their bodies dropped to the ground, all sprawled. They looked at each other, then at Leo, then at each other again with big, surprised eyes. They could not believe it. Leo had used his whisper voice with his teacher and had climbed another step of his Bravery Ladder! They pulled themselves up, turned in circles, and whimpered, "Oh no, oh no, this can't be happening! Oh no, oh no!"

Leo's Sneaky Fears stared at this new, strong and brave Leo. Then just before Leo's eyes, his Sneaky Fears slowly transformed into harmless, leashed little jackal puppies.

Leo's teacher was so proud of him. Leo smiled as he thought, *Just a few more steps to climb and I'll be at the top of my Bravery Ladder. That's when I'll be really brave and Sneaky Fears will be all tame!*

STORy ChapTeR 8.

A few weeks later, Leo felt so proud. **He felt so brave.** He felt like he was really the King of the Jungle!

Leo had finally climbed the very top step of his Bravery Ladder for Speaking at School. He had raised his paw and answered his teacher's question in front of all the animals in his class. And he had used his real roar to do it!

It had not been easy to climb all the way up to the top of his Bravery Ladder. It had been really, really hard work. In fact, it had taken Leo a few weeks to climb all the steps of his Bravery Ladder for Speaking at School.

Many times, Leo felt like he could not do it. Many times, his brain thought it was just too hard to climb all the way up his Bravery Ladder, so he should just give up. But Leo figured out that when his brain thought it was too hard to climb all the way up his Bravery Ladder and he should just give up, it was his Sneaky Fears playing tricks on him and sneaking scary thoughts in his brain. That was just his Sneaky Fears trying to be the boss of him!

Even when Leo got stuck on a step for a little while, and especially when he had trouble climbing that last, really hard step, he did not give up. Leo's mom and his teacher helped. They reminded him that he needed to keep at it and not give up if he wanted to tame his Sneaky Fears. Leo did not give up. He worked hard at climbing his Bravery Ladder and Taming Sneaky Fears.

And he did it!

Leo was now going on a play date at Ellie's house. He could not wait to tell her about how he had tamed his Sneaky Fears. His Sneaky Fears were following him with leashes on their necks, all tame, smelling of bubble bath soap. When Leo glanced at them, his Sneaky Fears looked up at him like quiet little jackal puppies waiting to be petted.

When Leo arrived at Ellie's house, he said hi to Ellie's mom with his real roar. Ellie's mom had been baking again. Leo's mouth watered and his tummy growled when he whiffed and saw freshly-baked cookies. Leo couldn't wait for snack time!

Leo was now able to use his real roar to say hi to lots of grown-up animals he trusted. As he rubbed his tummy, Leo told Ellie's mom, "It smells sooo good!" Then he ran upstairs to Ellie's room. Ellie's door was open and when Leo walked in, he came to a sudden halt.

Leo could not believe what he was seeing.

Ellie was sitting on the top bunk!

Ellie had climbed all the steps of the bunk bed ladder and was holding the present, still wrapped up in the pretty paper and ribbon and bow. Ellie's trunk was all the way up. Her eyes were sparkling with excitement. Her beautiful big ears were flapping. She was giggling and giggling. Next to her, there was a pretty purple cage covered with a hot pink cloth. Leo heard soft grumbling and saw long crooked fingers tapping and tapping impatiently under the hot pink cloth. Leo imagined that Missy Mistake was grumpy because she could not be the boss of Ellie any more.

Leo ran to the bunk bed and climbed all the way up, with his tamed Sneaky Fears behind him. Ellie's eyes could not stop sparkling as she smiled at Leo and started unwrapping the present she had been waiting so long to get.

As Leo watched Ellie and her Missy Mistake's pretty purple cage under the hot pink cloth, he smiled. Leo thought that he and Ellie each had the best and most precious gifts of all: a best friend, and tamed Sneaky Fears!

THE END

PaRT B.

WORKBOOK: iNside Leo the LiON's Den – How to Tame YouR SNeaky FeaRs

WORKBOOK SECTION 1.
Be The Boss of Your Body

Welcome to Leo's den! I'm Leo's mom. Leo, who is standing right next to me, is too shy to use his voice to welcome you to his den today so he asked me to do it for him. I told Leo that I would do the welcome today, but after today, Leo will need to use his own voice. Even shy, nervous, and scared animals need to use their voice to speak!

Leo was just about to start drawing. Along with Leo, why don't you draw a picture of what your body feels and looks like when you're feeling happy? Use the body outline on the next page to make your drawing. If you're not too sure about how your body feels and looks like when you're feeling happy, you could do charades with your family to figure it out. Make sure you figure out what each part of your body feels and looks like when you feel happy; including your face and neck, the muscles of your legs, arms, and shoulders, and the inside of your body—like your heart and tummy and lungs (or breathing).

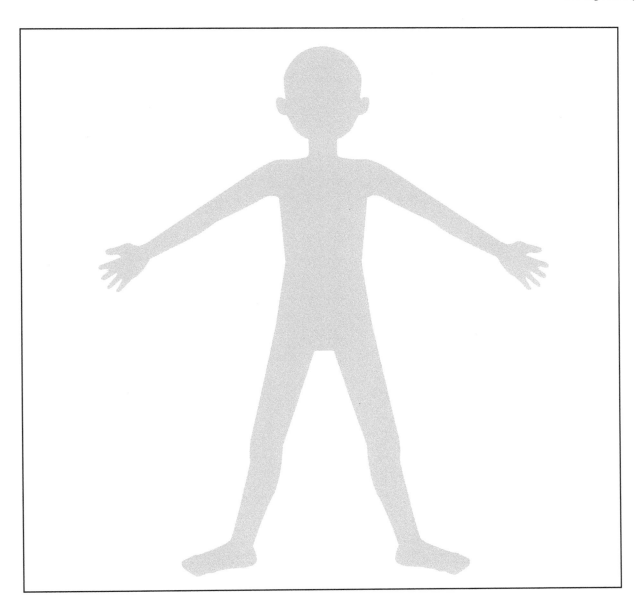

My Body Scan for Happy

When you look at the clues each part of your body gives you when you feel something, you're doing a Body Scan! Just like Leo is learning how to do a Body Scan with you right now. Doing a Body Scan is the first thing you need to do to be the boss of your body. When you're the boss of your body, you can make your body calm down even if your body doesn't want to calm down!

Now, draw a picture of what your body feels and looks like when you're mad or angry. Do a Body Scan for mad or angry. That means, figure out what each part of your body feels and looks like when you're mad or angry, including your face and neck, the muscles of your legs, arms, and shoulders, and the inside of your body like your heart and tummy and lungs (or breathing). If you're not sure how your body feels and looks when you're mad or angry, you could do charades with your family to figure it out. Use the body outline on the next page to make your drawing.

My Body Scan for Mad or Angry

Before you came to Leo's den today, Leo and I decided that I would show you one thing that you can do to be the boss of your body and make your body relax, just like Leo did in the story. All you need to do is Spaghetti Arms and Toes. When you do Spaghetti Arms and Toes you make your muscles and your body relax, even if your body doesn't want to relax. Spaghetti Arms and Toes makes you the boss of your body!

Practice Spaghetti Arms and Toes with your parent right now, while Leo practices with me. Make sure to lie down on your back and close your eyes. Your parent will dim the lights and then read the same thing I'll be reading to Leo.

Spaghetti Arms and Toes Script (parent to read):

Close your eyes and pay attention to how your muscles feel in your body. Pretend that your toes and feet are like uncooked spaghetti, and stretch and tighten up your toes and feet as tight as you can. Hold them tight as you count to five slowly—one, two, three, four, five. Feel how hard the muscles in your toes and feet feel. Your muscles feel a little sore because they're so hard and stiff. Now pretend your toes and feet are going in warm water, and let them loosen up. Feel how soft and relaxed the muscles in your toes and feet feel. Your muscles feel nice and they're not sore anymore.

Now tighten up your whole legs and thighs. Make both of your legs and thighs really tight and stiff and count to five slowly—one, two, three, four, five. Feel how hard the muscles in your legs and thighs feel. Your muscles feel a little sore because they're so stiff. Now your whole legs and thighs are going in the warm water and you can let them loosen up. Feel how soft and relaxed the muscles in your legs and thighs feel. Your muscles feel soft and relaxed and they're not sore anymore.

Now hold your arms, your hands, and your fingers out in front of you really stiff, just like uncooked spaghetti. Hold them really stiff as you count to five slowly—one, two, three, four, five. Feel how hard the muscles in your arms, hands, and fingers feel. Your muscles feel a little sore because they're so stiff. Now they're going in the warm water and you can let them loosen up. Feel how soft and relaxed the muscles in your arms, hands, and fingers feel. Your muscles feel soft and relaxed and they're not sore anymore.

Now scrunch up your face and try to tighten your shoulders so your shoulders touch your ears. Make the muscles in your face and shoulders really stiff and tight and count to five slowly—one, two, three, four, five. Feel how hard the muscles in your face and shoulders feel. The muscles in your face and neck feel a little sore because they're so stiff and you might even have a bit of a headache. Now the muscles in your face and neck are going in the warm water and becoming loose and relaxed. Feel how soft and relaxed the muscles in your face and neck feel. Your muscles feel soft and relaxed and they're not sore anymore.

Now pretend your whole body is a giant uncooked spaghetti noodle, all hard and stiff. Tighten up your legs and feet and toes and arms and hands and fingers and your whole body, including your face and neck—and even your back and tummy. Hold everything really stiff and count to five slowly—one, two, three, four, five. Feel how hard the muscles in your whole body feel. Your muscles feel a little sore because they're so stiff. You might even feel your tummy is getting sore. Now your whole body is going into the warm water and getting really soft and relaxed.

Doesn't Spaghetti Arms and Toes make your body feel good? My Leo just whispered to me that his muscles feel soft and relaxed. Practice Spaghetti Arms and Toes five more times so you become really good at using it. Leo and I will do the same, and we'll see you in Leo's den soon!

WORKBOOK SECTION 2.
Be The Boss of Your Body... and Your Brain!

Leo's mother is smiling as she says, "Hello there! My brave Leo had such a good night's sleep. Leo just did Spaghetti Arms and Toes so his body feels relaxed right now. Leo wants to use his voice to welcome you to his den today. Go on, Leo, remember, even shy animals need to use their voice."

With a shy smile on his face, Leo says, "Hi. I'm Leo. Today, I decided to be brave and use my voice to welcome you to my den, just like I promised when you came to my den last time. I'm so happy that you want to learn to be brave, just like I do. Let's meet in my den every time you read a new chapter of my story. Together we can practice what I learn in my story. That way, we'll learn how to be brave together! It'll be like our own private Bravery Club!"

"Leo, that's a great idea," Leo's mother tells him. She continues, "Leo was about to draw, so with your parent, why don't you do the same as Leo and I are going to do? Draw a Body Scan of what your body feels like and looks like when you're nervous and scared. If you're not sure how your body feels and looks when you're nervous and scared, you could do charades with your family to figure it out. Just like Leo, pay close attention to what each part of your body feels and looks like when you're feeling nervous and scared—including your face and neck, the muscles of your legs, arms and shoulders, and the inside of your body; like your heart and tummy and lungs (or breathing). Use the body outline on the next page to make your drawing.

My Body Scan for Nervous or Scared

"Now, just like Leo is doing, draw a Body Scan of what your body feels and looks like when you're shy. If you're not sure how your body feels and looks when you're shy, you could do charades with your family to figure it out. Remember to pay attention to what each part of your body feels and looks like when you're feeling shy, including your face and neck, the muscles of your legs, arms and shoulders, and the inside of your body—like your heart and tummy and lungs (or breathing). Use the body outline on the next page to draw your Body Scan for shy.

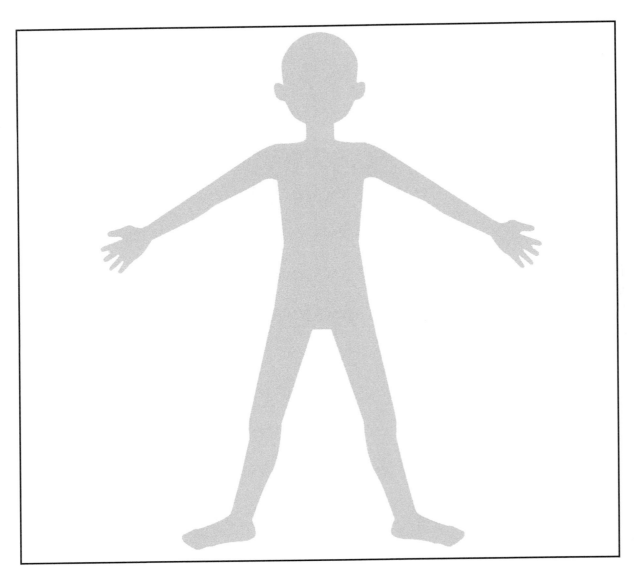

My Body Scan for Shy

"Later, you and your parents could draw more Body Scans using the extra body outlines for what your body feels and looks like when you have other feelings like sad, embarrassed, and any other feelings you can think of. You could even play charades to figure out how your body feels and looks like with lots of different feelings. Playing charades can be a lot of fun to figure out feelings. You'll see that your body feels and looks different when you have different feelings. If you do Body Scans and pay close attention to what your body feels and looks like when you're feeling something, then you'll be able to figure out if you're feeling happy, nervous and scared; or calm, safe and relaxed; or sad, angry, or shy; or any other feeling.

My Body Scan for _____

My Body Scan for _____

"Now, practice Balloon Breathing with your parent while Leo and I do the same. Make sure you lie down on your back. Your parent will give you a small toy or puppet. Put it on your tummy and you'll give it a slow ride up and down while you do Balloon Breathing, just like Leo the Lion and his baby sister Lilly did in the story.

Your parent will read the same words that I'll be reading to Leo, so that you and Leo can practice Balloon Breathing at the same time. Close your eyes and focus on your breathing and your heart and your tummy."

Balloon Breathing Script (parent to read):

Take a slow breath in through your nose and let your tummy move up as you count to five slowly—one, two, three, four, five. Now slowly let out your breath through your mouth and let your tummy come down. Do that again. Take a breath in through your nose and let your tummy rise up while you count to five slowly—one, two, three, four, five. Now slowly breathe out through your mouth. Do this five more times, really slowly. Make sure your shoulders and chest don't move at all, and that only your belly moves up and down really slowly when you do Balloon Breathing.

Leo's mom says, "Doing Balloon Breathing feels good, doesn't it? Now as you practice Balloon Breathing, your parent will help you do Imagery at the same time. Just like Leo and I are going to do with you. That will really make you and Leo feel nice and relaxed."

Imagery Script (parent to read):

Close your eyes and pretend or imagine that you're lying on a beach on a beautiful sunny day. Imagine the bright yellow sun shining. You see fluffy white clouds in the blue sky. The sun is warm and feels so good on your skin. You hear the soft whisper of a gentle breeze. The air smells fresh and clean. The white sand is warm and soft and feels really, really good. You can hear the waves coming in and going out. The sound of the waves makes you feel safe, calm, and relaxed. You think about building a sand castle, but right now it feels so good to just lie here on the soft, warm sand. You let the bright sun shine on you. You hear the waves come in and go out. You feel safe, warm, comfortable, and so relaxed. Just imagine for a few more minutes the fluffy white clouds in the blue sky as they float by above you, the soft sound of the waves, the feel of the warm sun on your skin, and the smell of the salty, clean sea air. Now slowly open our eyes.

Leo's mom says, "Notice what your brain is thinking after you've done Imagery. Your brain is probably thinking nice thoughts because *you* made your brain think nice thoughts! That means when you do Imagery, you're the boss of your brain! And when you do Balloon Breathing and Imagery together, you're the boss of your body and the boss of your brain!

"Just like Leo is going to do now, draw a picture of the calm and safe place you want your brain to think about when you're the boss of your brain and do Imagery. Make sure to draw what you see, what you hear, what you smell, what you feel inside your body, what you feel on your skin, and even what you taste and what movements your body makes when you're in your own calm and safe place. Use the space on the next page to make your drawing of your calm and safe place.

MY SAFE AND CALM PLACE
WHEN I DO IMAGERY

"Now, just like Leo is doing, do a Body Scan of what your body feels and looks like when you're feeling calm and relaxed. If you're not sure how your body feels and looks when you're calm and relaxed, you could do charades with your family to figure it out. Remember to pay attention to what each part of your body feels and looks like when you're feeling calm and relaxed, including your face and neck, the muscles of your legs, arms and shoulders, and the inside of your body; like your heart and tummy and lungs (or breathing). Use the body outline below to draw your Body Scan for calm and relaxed.

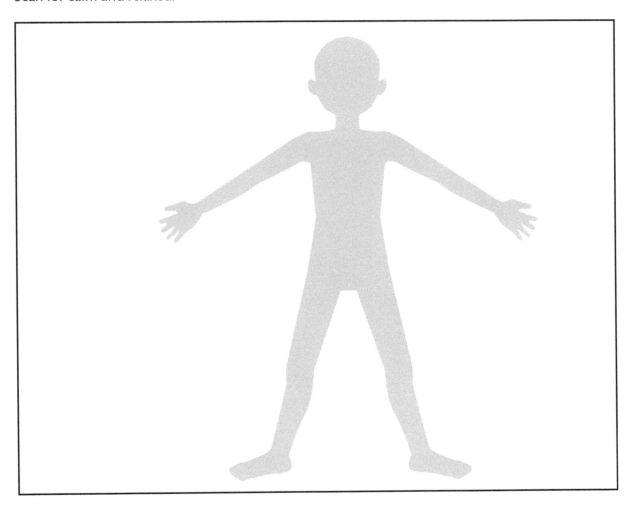

My Body Scan for Calm and Relaxed

"You and Leo are working so hard! I'm really proud of you both! Just like Leo, practice doing Spaghetti Arms and Toes, Balloon Breathing, and Imagery *at two different times every day*. You can practice with your parents and even on your own like Leo does every day! Make sure you practice *when your body doesn't need to calm down*. Remember to practice doing Spaghetti Arms and Toes, Balloon Breathing, and Imagery every day, even when you don't need to. That way, when you need to calm your body really fast, Spaghetti Arms and Toes, Balloon Breathing, and Imagery will work really well!

"Well, I think we're all done for today. Oh, wait a minute. Leo wants to say something. Go on Leo."

"My body feels calm and relaxed right now, Mom," Leo says with a soft roar.

"That's because you did Spaghetti Arms and Toes, Balloon Breathing, and Imagery, Leo," his mom tells him.

Leo smiles as he says, "I really like how my body feels when I'm calm and relaxed. Bye! See you in my den next time."

WORKBOOK SECTION 3.
Discover Your Own Sneaky Fears

Hi there! It's me, Leo the Lion. I just did Spaghetti Arms and Toes, Balloon Breathing, and Imagery and so I'm feeling brave enough to use my soft voice to speak with you and I'm going to talk all by myself today. I'm so happy that you came back to my den because that means we're becoming friends. Now we can work together to learn how to be brave, and tame our Sneaky Fears! If you're like me, I bet you didn't know that Sneaky Fears like to bother lots and lots of kids.

If your own Sneaky Fears are as scary and wild and stinky as mine, your Sneaky Fears really need taming! Each time we meet in my den, we'll learn how to be brave and tame our Sneaky Fears! My mom said it's going to be hard to tame Sneaky Fears, but lots and lots of animals and kids have learned to be brave and have tamed their Sneaky Fears. Let's start right away!

In the story, you saw what my Sneaky Fears look and smell like, and what scary and untrue thoughts they keep sneaking in my brain to make me feel shy and scared and nervous, and make my throat feel all squeezed so my voice won't come out. Draw a picture of what your own Sneaky Fears look like when they sneak scary and untrue thoughts in your brain to make you feel shy or nervous and scared, or squeeze your throat so your voice gets stuck and won't come out. Use the space on the next page to do your drawing.

MY OWN
SNEAKY FEARS

If you decide to choose a pet name for your own Sneaky Fears, print the name on your picture (or have your parent help you print it). When you give your Sneaky Fears a pet name, that makes them a little less scary, so go ahead and decide what name you'd like to give your own Sneaky Fears. If you want to name them "Sneaky Fears," that's okay.

Now draw a picture of your own Sneaky Fears using their first trick of Not Telling the Truth. Use the space below to do your drawing. Make sure to also do a Body Scan of what your body looks and feels like when your Sneaky Fears are using that first trick! You can use the body outline to draw what your body looks and feels like when Sneaky Fears use their first trick of Not Telling the Truth.

My Sneaky Fears Using the Trick Not Telling the Truth

Now draw a picture of you using the first two Trick Stoppers, Ignore Sneaky Fears and Think Brave Thoughts. Use the space below to do your drawing. Make sure to do a Body Scan of what your body looks and feels like after you use the Trick Stoppers. You can use the body outline on the next page to draw what your body looks and feels like.

I AM USING MY FIRST TWO TRICK STOPPERS

IGNORE SNEAKY FEARS   AND   THINK BRAVE THOUGHTS

I really, really want to tame my Sneaky Fears! That's why I practice Spaghetti Arms and Toes, Balloon Breathing, and Imagery every day, even when I don't need to. That way they will work really well and really fast when I need them!

I decided that I was going to be a Trick Catcher and use my Trick Stoppers every single day!

I hope you'll do all of that too. It's going to be great when our Sneaky Fears quit bothering us! I already started taming my own Sneaky Fears: I was able to smile at Ellie in the Club and I'm able to speak to you now because I used Spaghetti Arms and Toes, Balloon Breathing, and Imagery, and because I was a Trick Catcher and used my Trick Stoppers. That means I'm slowly Taming my Sneaky Fears! I'm happy you're doing it too!

Let's meet again real soon. I can't wait to see what happens next in my story!

WORKBOOK SECTION 4.
Be the Boss of Your Brain

Hi there! It's me, Leo the Lion, all by myself again. I'm so happy that I've made two new friends; Ellie the Elephant and you. And I'm proud of being able to use my real voice not just with you, but also with Ellie. I've been practicing Spaghetti Arms and Toes, Balloon Breathing, and Imagery every day and they really work! I'm also trying to be a good Trick Catcher and use the Trick Stoppers every time I catch Sneaky Fears playing tricks on my brain. I bet you're doing the same. Let's get started and I'll show you what I learned about how to tame our Sneaky Fears!

Just like I'm going to do now: Draw two pictures; one that shows your Sneaky Fears using the trick Exaggerating, and another picture that shows your Sneaky Fears using the trick Only Showing the Bad Things. Use the space on the next page to do your drawing.

MY SNEAKY FEARS
USING THE TRICK EXAGGERATING

MY SNEAKY FEARS
ONLY SHOWING THE BAD THINGS

I'm also going to draw a Body Scan of how my body feels nervous and scared when my Sneaky Fears use these tricks. Make sure you do the same. Use the body outline below to do your drawing.

My Body Scan for Nervous and Scared When My Sneaky Fears Use Their Tricks

Just like I'm doing now, draw a picture of you using your new Trick Stopper, Talk to an Adult. Use the space on the next page to do your drawing. Make sure you also draw a Body Scan of how your body feels nice and calm when you use your new Trick Stopper. Use the body outline on the next page to do your drawing.

I'M USING MY TRICK STOPPERS

TALK TO AN ADULT

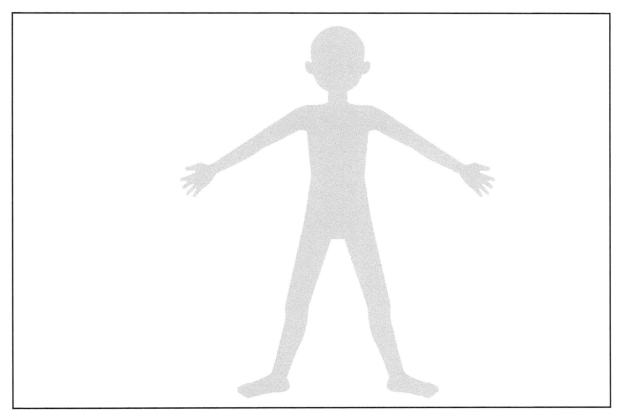

Now, just like I'm going to do, make a list of all the adults you trust that you could talk to when you use your Trick Stopper, Talk to an Adult. Use the space below to draw pictures of these adults and have your mom and dad help you write their names.

I CAN TALK TO _____

Look carefully at your Body Scans of how your body feels when Sneaky Fears use their tricks. Do you see how yucky your body feels whenever Sneaky Fears use their tricks?

Now look at the Body Scans of how your body feels after you use your three Trick Stoppers to stop your Sneaky Fears. Look at your drawings of the Body Scans you did last time we met in my den, the drawings of how your body felt after you used the first two Trick Stoppers, Ignore Sneaky Fears and Think Brave Thoughts. And look at the drawing you just made of how your body feels after you used the third Trick Stopper, Talk to an Adult. See how calm and relaxed your body feels after you use your Trick Stoppers.

When you use the three Trick Stoppers and Spaghetti Arms and Toes, Balloon Breathing, and Imagery, *you are* the boss of your body and brain and you don't let Sneaky Fears be the boss. That means, you're slowly Taming Sneaky Fears!

Make sure you don't let your Sneaky Fears make you want to give up. It takes a lot of time to tame them because they don't give up easily. Lots and lots of animals and kids have been able to tame their Sneaky Fears. We can too!

WORKBOOK SECTION 5.
Discover Your Own Feeling Thermometer

Hi again! Welcome back to my den. I was a little nervous about speaking to you today, so I was just doing Balloon Breathing and Imagery to make my body all calm and relaxed. And it worked! I feel calm and relaxed enough now that I can use my voice to speak with you. I'm really glad you're here today. I have to tell you, Ellie's mom's cupcakes were delicious!

I'm so proud of myself because I'm working hard at Taming my Sneaky Fears and speaking more and more with my real voice. It's great!

Ellie and I really like the idea of a Feeling Thermometer. I hope you like it too. Just like Ellie and I did when we were eating our cupcakes at her house, let's draw three pictures today. You can use the Feeling Thermometer for Nervous or Scared on the next page that Ellie and I drew just for you.

The first thing to draw is a picture of something that makes you just a little nervous or scared, like at a 1 or 2 on your Feeling Thermometer for Nervous or Scared. You could ask your parent to help you remember a time if you have trouble remembering. Then, right next to your drawing, in the body outline for the 1 or 2, draw a Body Scan of how your body feels when you're nervous or scared at a 1 or 2. Use the space and body outline on the next page to do your drawing.

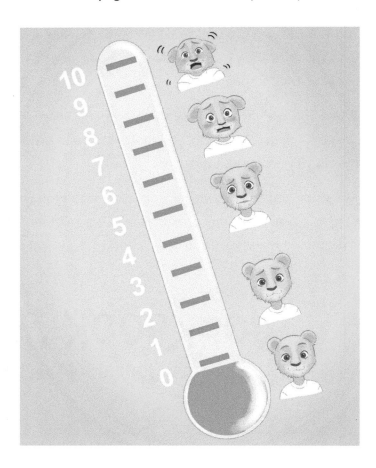

Now draw another picture of a time when your body felt nervous or scared at a 4 or 5 on your Feeling Thermometer for Nervous or Scared. Use the space on the next page to do your drawing. You could ask your parent to help you remember a time if you have trouble remembering. Then, in the body outline next to your drawing, draw a Body Scan of what your body feels and looks like when you're nervous or scared at a 4 or 5 on your Feeling Thermometer for Nervous or Scared. You could do charades to help you remember.

Now, draw something that makes your body feel really nervous or scared all the way up to a 9 or 10 on your Feeling Thermometer for Nervous or Scared. Use the space on the next page to do your drawing. You could ask your parent to help you remember a time if you'd like. When you're done, draw in the body outline next to it a Body Scan of what your body feels and looks like when you're nervous or scared all the way up to a 9 or 10 on your Feeling Thermometer for Nervous or Scared.

My Feeling Thermometer for Nervous or Scared

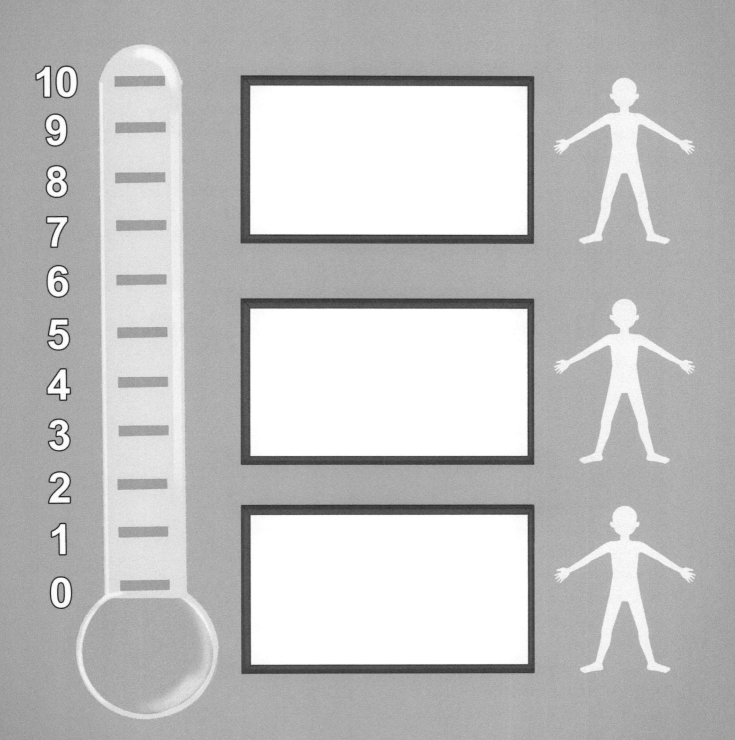

Ellie and I decided to use our Feeling Thermometer every day to figure out how nervous or scared our bodies feel. That way, we can become really, really good at being a Feeling Catcher and using the Feeling Thermometer. I hope you do the same with us.

Ellie and I also decided to always pay attention to when we feel shy or nervous or scared at a 5 or more on the Feeling Thermometer. When that happens, that's *way* too high! When we're a 5 or more on the Feeling Thermometer, we have to do Spaghetti Arms and Toes, Balloon Breathing, and Imagery until our Feeling Thermometer gets all the way down to a 0 or a 1. Try it too. You'll see that when you make your body calm, your brain can think more clearly. And then you can do everything better—like sports, schoolwork, making friends, and everything else!

I need to make my brain think clearly if I want to be a good Trick Catcher, use the three Trick Stoppers, and tame my Sneaky Fears. And that's true for Ellie and you too.

If we keep working hard together, our Sneaky Fears don't stand a chance.

WORKBOOK SECTION 6.
Build Your Own Bravery Ladder

Hi again! My body feels so relaxed now because I just finished practicing Spaghetti Arms and Toes, Balloon Breathing, and Imagery. Today, I asked my mom to come to my den when I meet with you. That's because when I came back from my play date with Ellie, I told my mom about Ellie climbing two steps of her Bravery Ladder. I also told her that I'd like to build my own Bravery Ladder. My mom said that she knew how to build Bravery Ladders, and so she showed me how to build one. I'm going to tell you what my mom said, but I want to make sure I don't forget steps—so my mom will help me. Right, mom?

"That's right, Leo," his mom says, "Isn't it fantastic that Ellie pushed herself so hard to climb two steps of her Bravery Ladder?"

Leo says, "It is, and I want to be as brave as Ellie and climb steps of my own Bravery Ladder. I hope you want that too, my new friend. After you build your Bravery Ladder then you, Ellie, and I can all climb our Bravery Ladders, one baby step at a time, while we tame our Sneaky Fears."

Leo's mom says, "That's right, Leo. Tell your new friend how to build a Bravery Ladder. I'll help you if you need help."

Leo says, "Okay. Let's see. When you build your own Bravery Ladder, you can have as many steps as you want on it, but what works best is to have five or six steps. Right, Mom?"

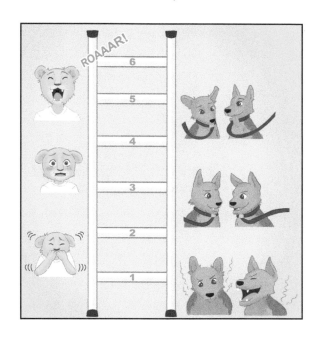

Leo's mom nods in agreement.

Leo continues, "First, you and your mom or dad need to decide what scares you, or makes you feel nervous or shy, and what you want to be brave about. It's like giving your Bravery Ladder a name. The name I gave my Bravery Ladder is My Bravery Ladder for Speaking at School. You or your mom or dad could write the name for your Bravery Ladder just above the drawing of your Bravery Ladder. Then, you and your mom or dad need to decide what you do now that shows you're scared or nervous or shy, and draw a picture of that at the bottom of your Bravery Ladder. I forgot the next part. What's next, Mom?"

Leo's mom says, "Leo, you're doing a great job explaining how to build a Bravery Ladder."

Leo says, "Thanks, Mom."

His mom continues, "Just like you're doing now, Leo, your new friend can use the space on the next page that has the drawing of a Bravery Ladder to make your picture. The next thing to do is to decide what you'll do when you've climbed to the top of your Bravery Ladder that shows you're brave, and you're not scared or nervous or shy anymore."

Leo says, "Just like I'm doing now, you can draw a picture of that at the top of the Bravery Ladder."

Leo's mom says, "Right. You and your new friend can use the space on the next page with the Bravery Ladder to make your drawing. Can you tell your new friend the next thing to do to build a Bravery Ladder, Leo?"

MY BRAVERY LADDER
FOR

Leo says, "Okay. You have to come up with five or six small baby steps that you're going to climb, slowly and one at a time, to go from the bottom of your Bravery Ladder all the way up to the top. You can ask your mom or dad's help to decide what each step might look like. Your mom or dad can write down what each step is going to be, or you can draw a picture of what you'll do at each step.

"Now, this is the best part. You and your mom or dad can come up with special points and rewards you'll get for climbing the steps. My mom and I decided to give me a chance to earn two points each time I climb a step. I get one point just for trying to climb the step, and one more point if I climb the step like I'm supposed to. After I get ten points, I get a really special reward—like deciding what movie we watch as a family on movie night, or going to the park to play with my mom or dad, or my favorite: getting an extra bedtime story! Each time I get ten more points, I get an even better reward. That makes me really want to climb more and more steps of my Bravery Ladder!"

Leo's mom says, "Leo, let's make a list of all the rewards you'll get every time you earn ten more points. Your friend and your friend's mom or dad could do the same. Let's use the space on the next page to make our list of rewards."

LIST OF MY REWARDS
FOR CLIMBING THE LADDER

Leo says, "I like the rewards that Mom and I put on my list. After you and your mom or dad have done all of that, you're ready to start climbing each step of your Bravery Ladder, just like Ellie did and like I'm going to start doing."

Leo's mom says, "Leo, you and your new friend will need to push yourselves to climb each step, especially the first step. That first step can be the hardest. What worked really well for Ellie, and what works really well for lots and lots of animals and kids is to do Spaghetti Arms and Toes, Balloon Breathing, and Imagery just before you're ready to climb a step. If you do that, your body is calm and relaxed and that makes it much easier for you to be the boss of your brain, Ignore your Sneaky Fears, and Think Brave Thoughts, like 'I can do it! I can climb that step! I can be the boss of my Sneaky Fears!' Remember, don't let your Sneaky Fears be the boss of you and sneak all sorts of untrue and scary thoughts in your brain. Use your three Trick Stoppers at each step."

Leo asks, "Mom, do I need to climb my Bravery Ladder every day?"

His mom says, "That's a great question, Leo. Climb one small step at a time, every day. You need to stay on each step for a little while. That means at least 20 minutes, but don't worry about the time, a grown-up will keep track of the time. You also need to climb a step of your Bravery Ladder at least four times every week. Don't worry about keeping track of the number of times. A grown-up will keep track."

Leo says, "Wow, I think that means I have to do lots of practice to climb the steps of my Bravery Ladder!"

Leo's mom says, "That's for sure. But remember the more you practice and climb the steps of a Bravery Ladder, the better it is and the easier it gets. If you, Ellie, and your new friend practice really hard, you all could become brave and tame your Sneaky Fears in just a few weeks!"

Leo says, "I'm ready to start climbing my Bravery Ladder!"

His mom says, "Great, Leo! I'll be cheering you and your new friend on!"

Leo says, "I'm really excited about my friend and me climbing each step of our own Bravery Ladder, just like Ellie. I know we can all do it! Bye for now from both my mom and me. See you next time!"

WORKBOOK SECTION 7.
Keep Climbing Your Bravery Ladder

Hi again! I'm glad you've come to see me in my den again today. Like I do everyday, I've just practiced my Spaghetti Arms and Toes, Balloon Breathing, and Imagery.

Can you believe it? I used my whisper voice with my teacher and climbed two steps of my Bravery Ladder for Speaking at school! I never thought I'd be able to do that. And look, I'm using my normal roar to speak with you right now. I feel so brave! I'm getting closer and closer to completely taming my Sneaky Fears!

I had to push myself a lot. You always have to push yourself to climb new steps on your Bravery Ladder, even if they're baby steps. That's because your Sneaky Fears are not fully tame until you've climbed all the way up to the top of your Bravery Ladder. Ellie could climb steps of her Bravery Ladder. I could too. You can do it too! All of us can climb new steps of our Bravery Ladders. We just need to remember to be the boss of our body and the boss of our brain as we're climbing each step.

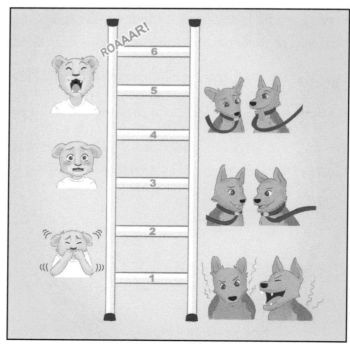

You could draw an X on your Bravery Ladder to show what step you're working on right now. And draw a picture of the next two steps you'll be climbing. Use the Bravery Ladder on the next page to do your drawing. Talk with your mom or dad about what you'll do to make sure you climb those next steps. Doing Spaghetti Arms and Toes, Balloon Breathing, and Imagery before you climb a step of your Bravery Ladder really helps. When you think you can't climb a step, that's just Sneaky Fears trying to be the boss of you and your brain by playing their three tricks. Don't let your Sneaky Fears be the boss of you as you're climbing the steps of your Bravery Ladder.

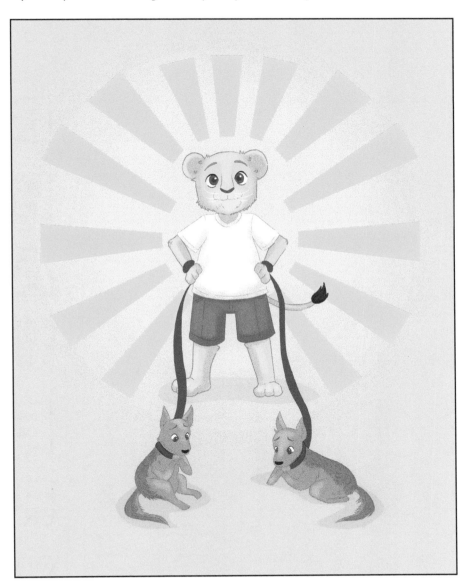

I know we can do it!
It's going to feel great when we've climbed
all the way up to the top step of our

Bravery Ladder!

THE NEXT TWO STEPS I'LL BE CLIMBING

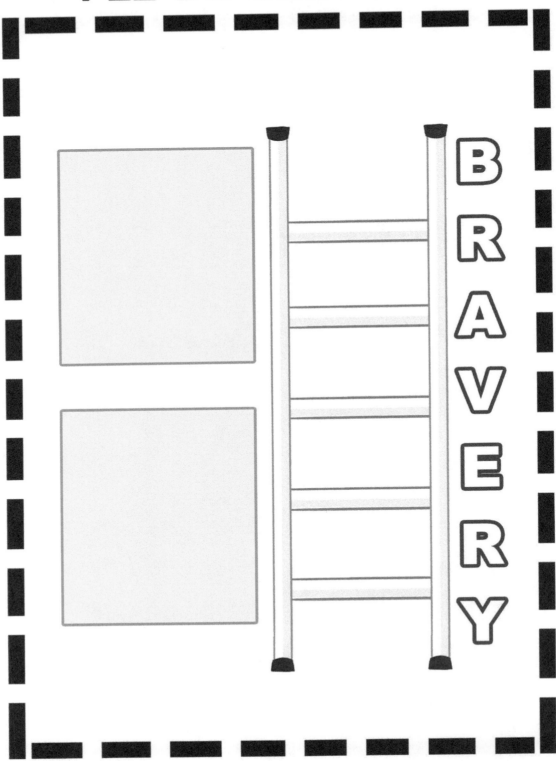

WORKBOOK SECTION 8.
You're Taming Your Sneaky Fears

Hi there! Ellie and I did it! We climbed all the way up our Bravery Ladders! Have you climbed all the way up your Bravery Ladder too?

If yes, BRAVO!!!!

If no, don't give up! Each step you climb brings you closer and closer to being really brave and Taming your Sneaky Fears! It's a great feeling when you've climbed all the way up your Bravery Ladder! Keep at it! Keep practicing Spaghetti Arms and Toes, Balloon Breathing, and Imagery every day. And keep being a Trick Catcher and use your Trick Stoppers to tame your Sneaky Fears.

Draw a picture of you with your tamed Sneaky Fears when you've climbed all the way up your Bravery Ladder. Use the space on the next page to do your drawing.

I'm really proud of myself, Ellie, and you, because we're working to tame our Sneaky Fears. Our Sneaky Fears need to know:

We won't give up!

About the Authors

Dr. Diane Benoit and Dr. Suneeta Monga are child psychiatrists at the Toronto Hospital for Sick Children and the University of Toronto. They work with young children to overcome their anxiety while giving their parents the resources to help.

Dr. Benoit's and Dr. Monga's work in developing the "Taming Sneaky Fears" treatment program inspired them to write the children's story and companion workbook, Taming Sneaky Fears. They recognized the lack of current, user-friendly resources and so collaborated to provide instructions on how to cope with anxiety. With more than a decade of feedback from children, parents, and therapists, they refined Leo's story and ensured the activities presented in the workbook can be put into practice by young children.

CPSIA information can be obtained
at www.ICGtesting.com
Printed in the USA
LVHW072030231118
597867LV00020B/542/P